C O M P L I C A T E D
SPIDERS
ANTI-STRESS COLORING BOOK

ILLUSTRATED BY
ANTONY BRIGGS

THIS BOOK BELONGS TO

..........anony.............

COMPLICATED
COLORING
www.complicatedcoloring.com

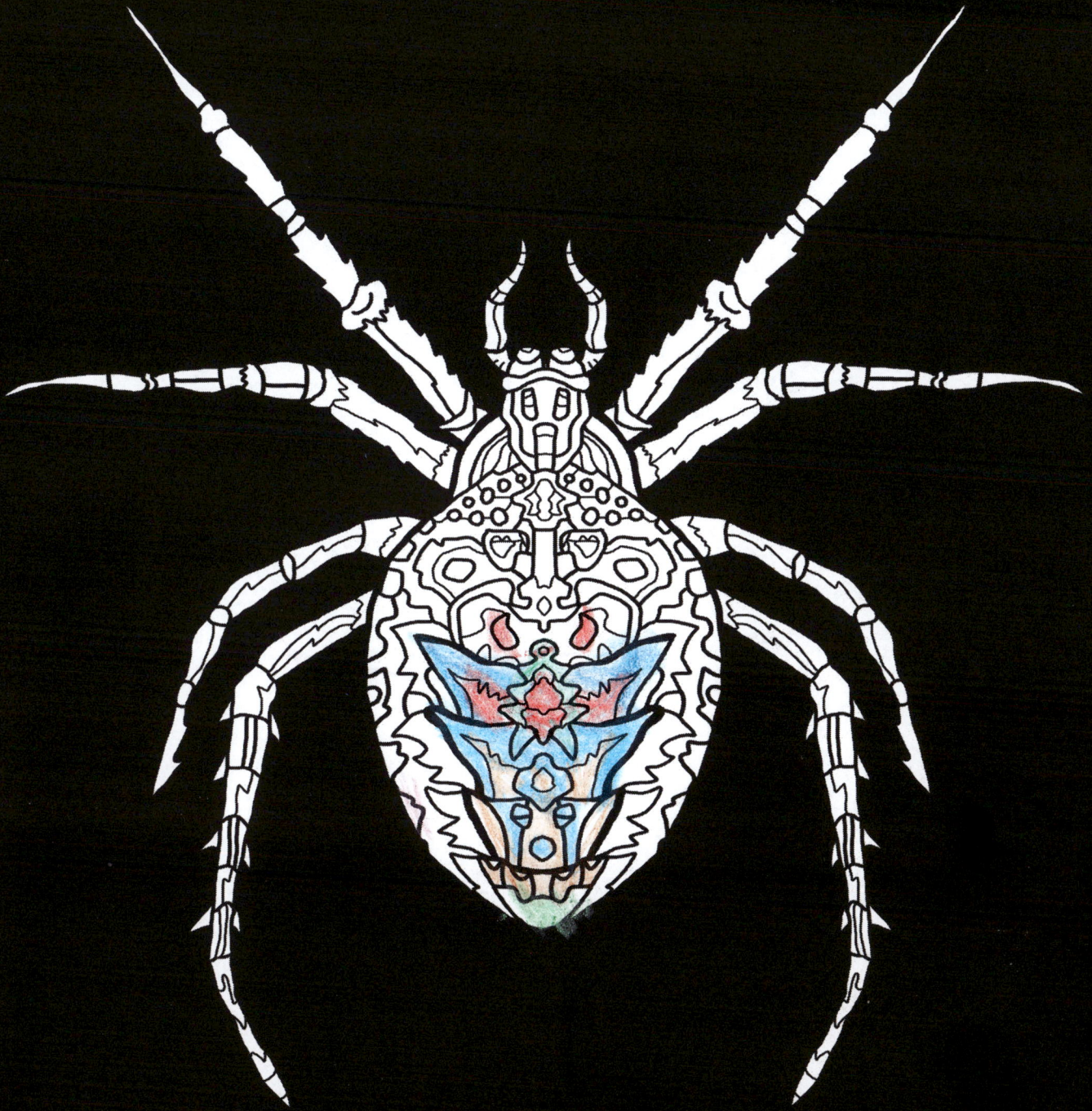

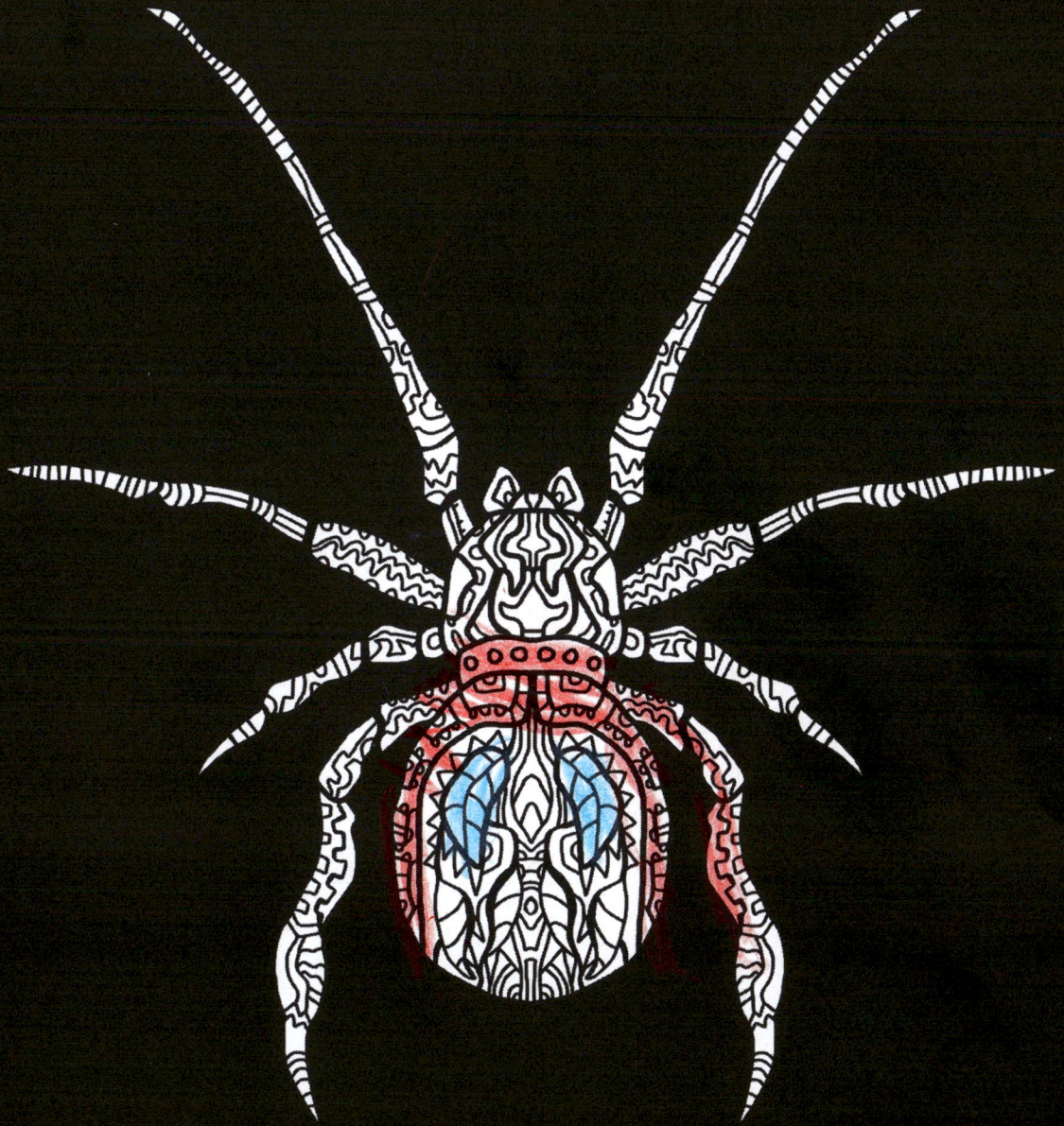

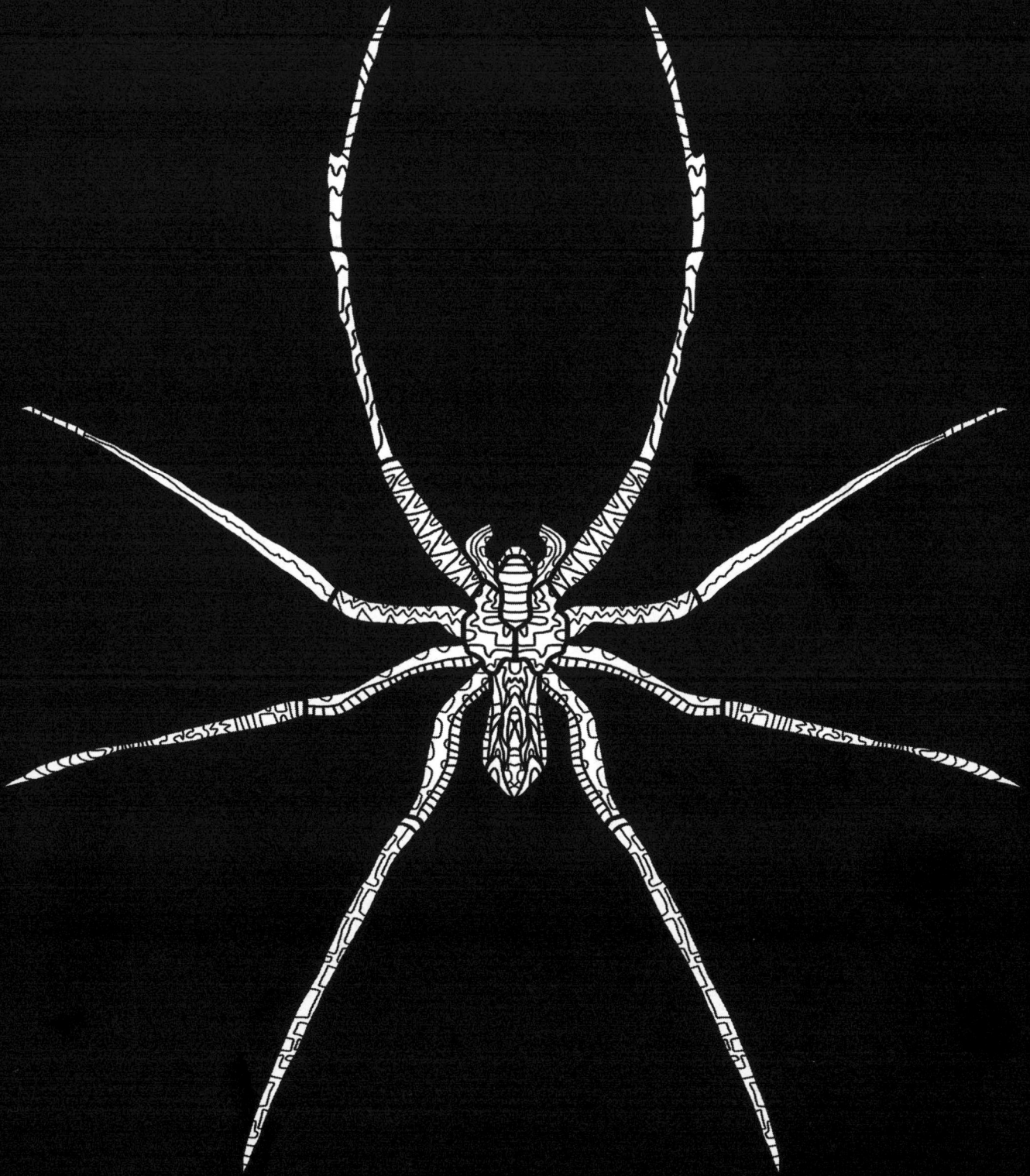

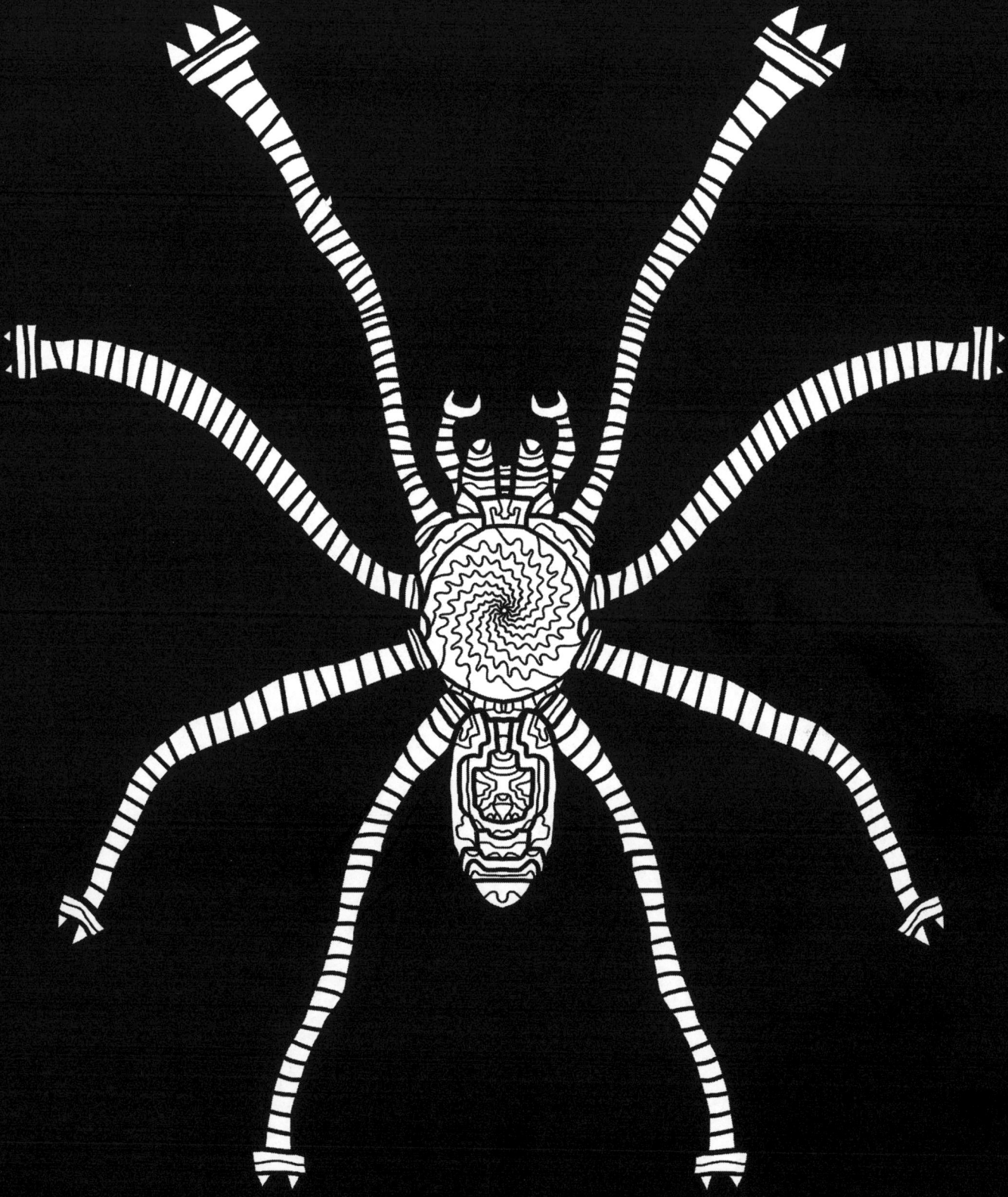

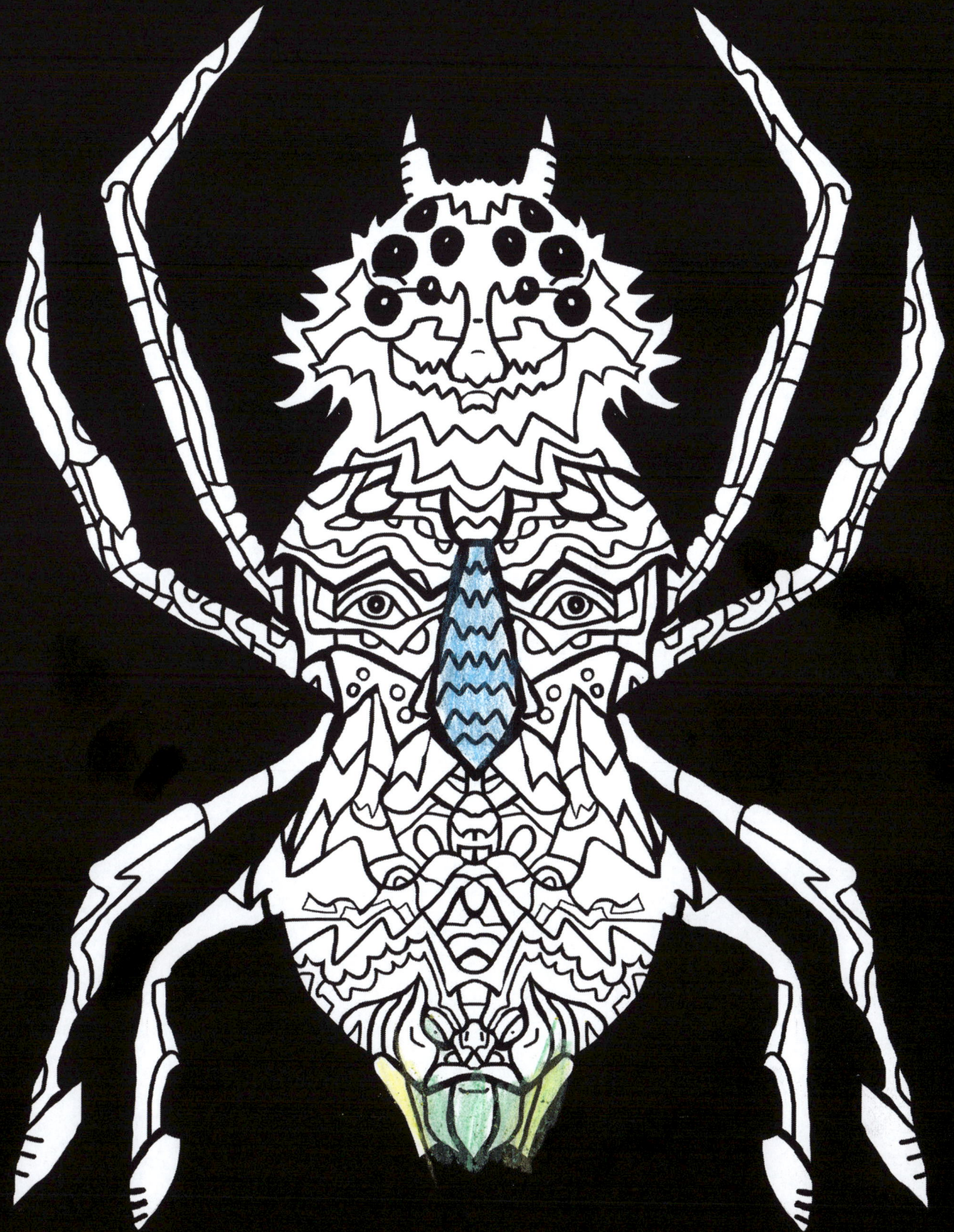

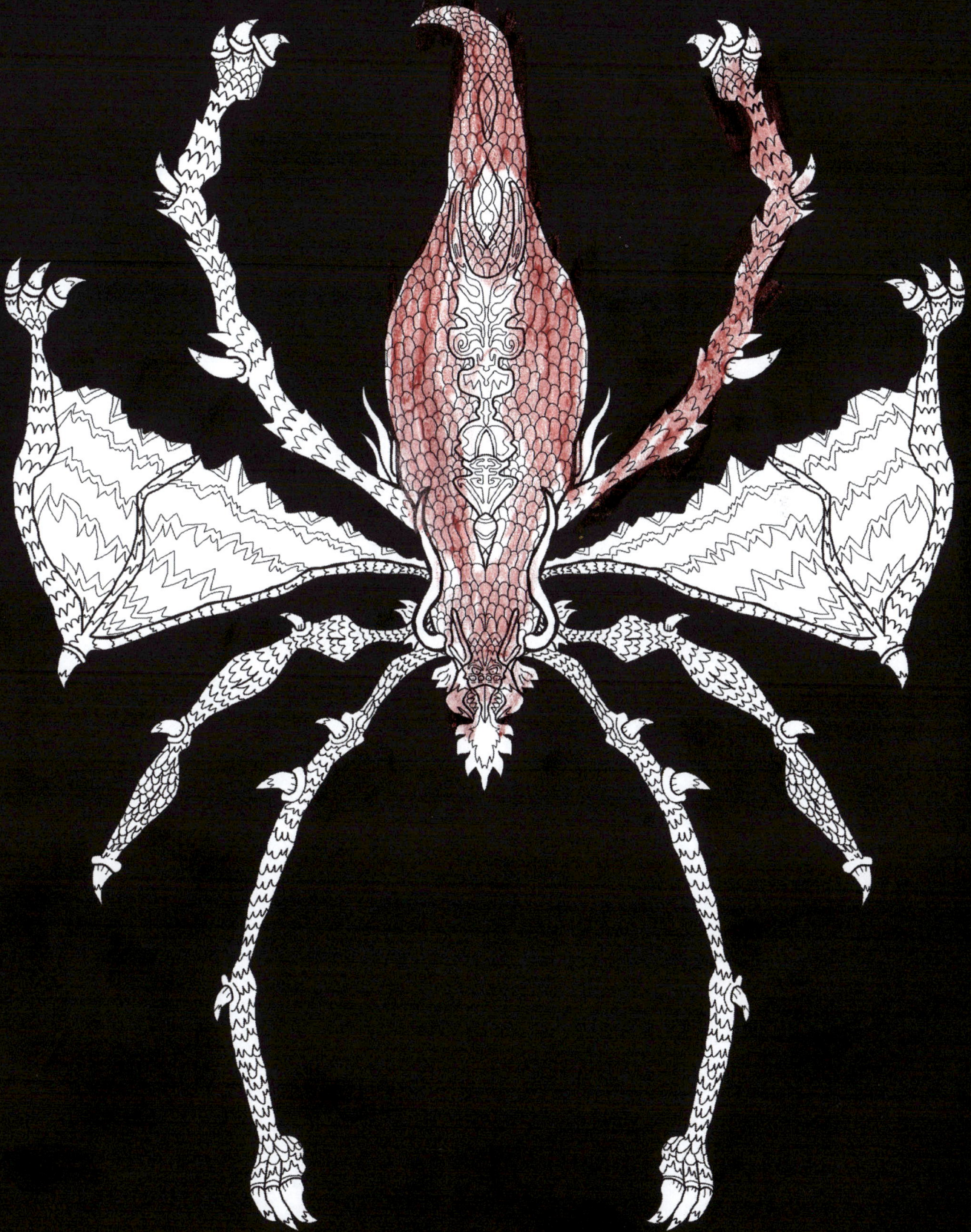

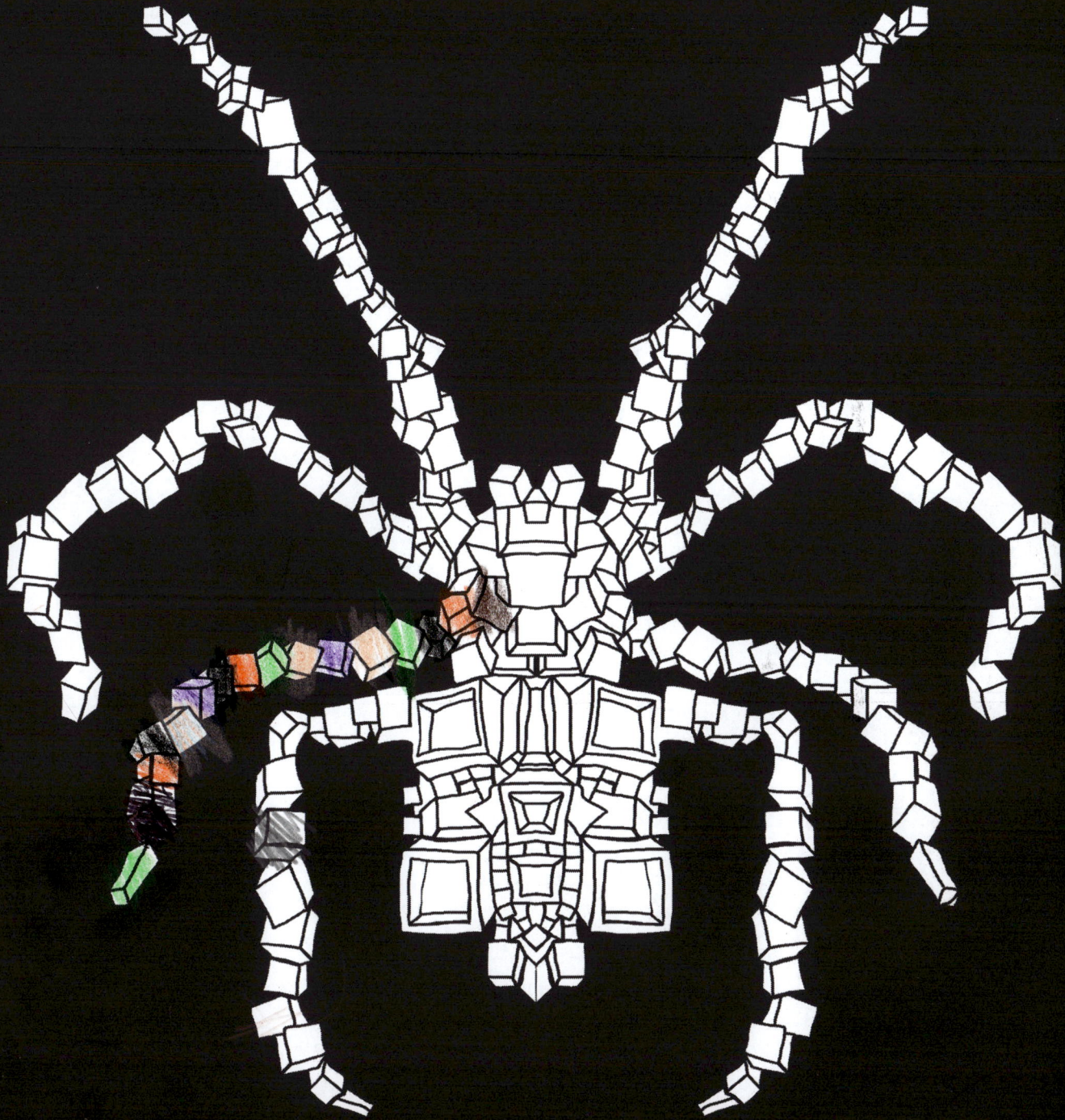

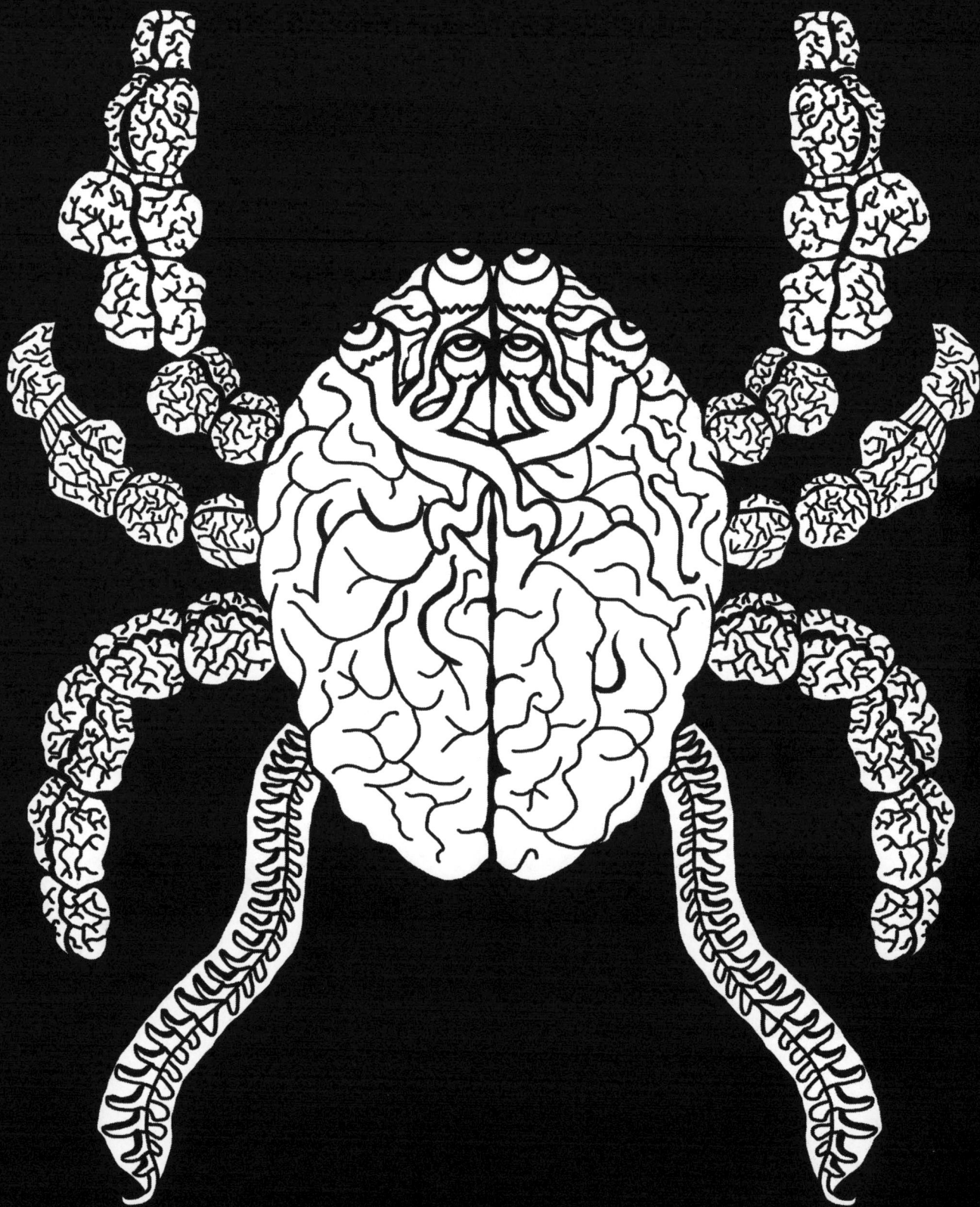

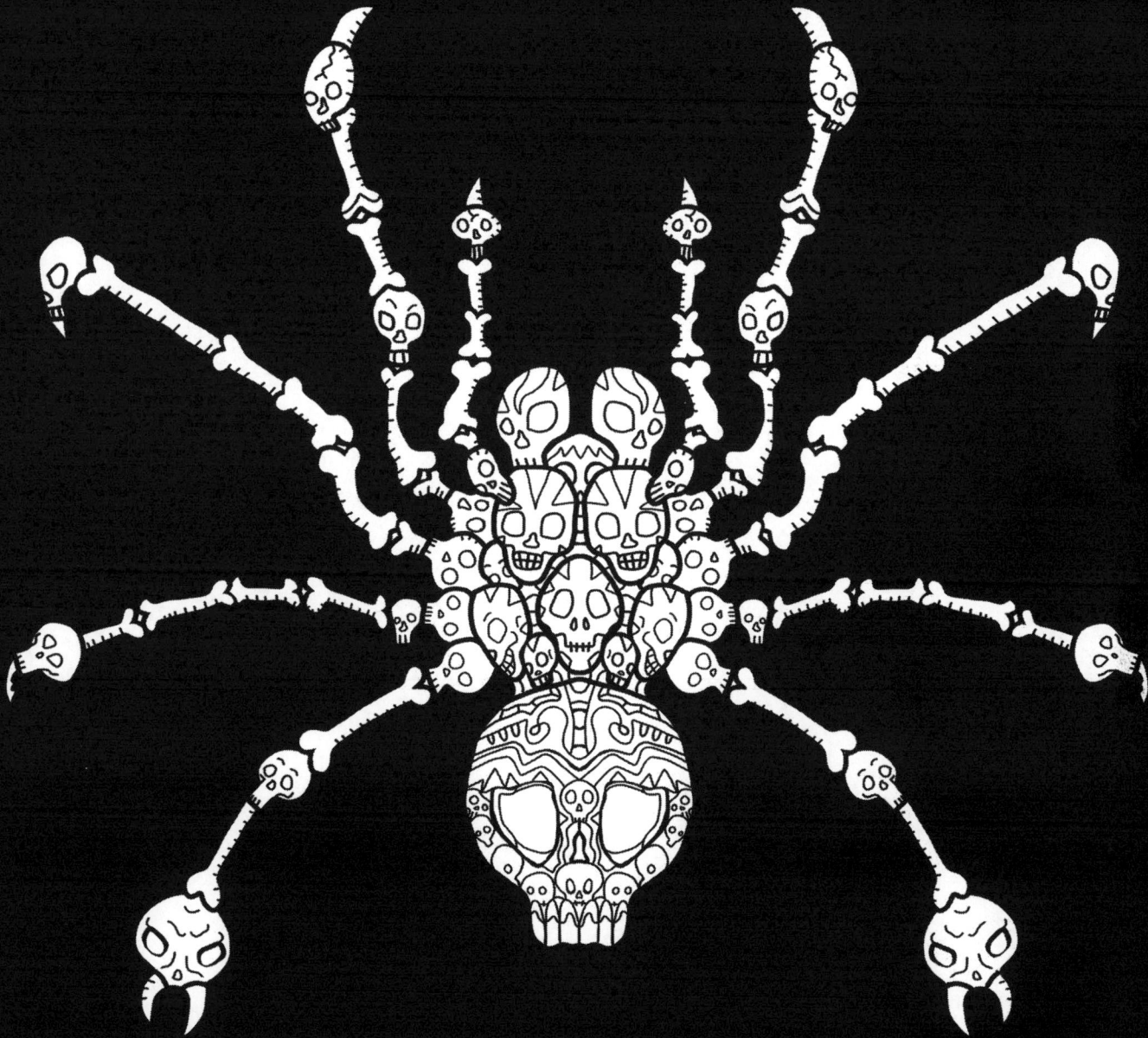

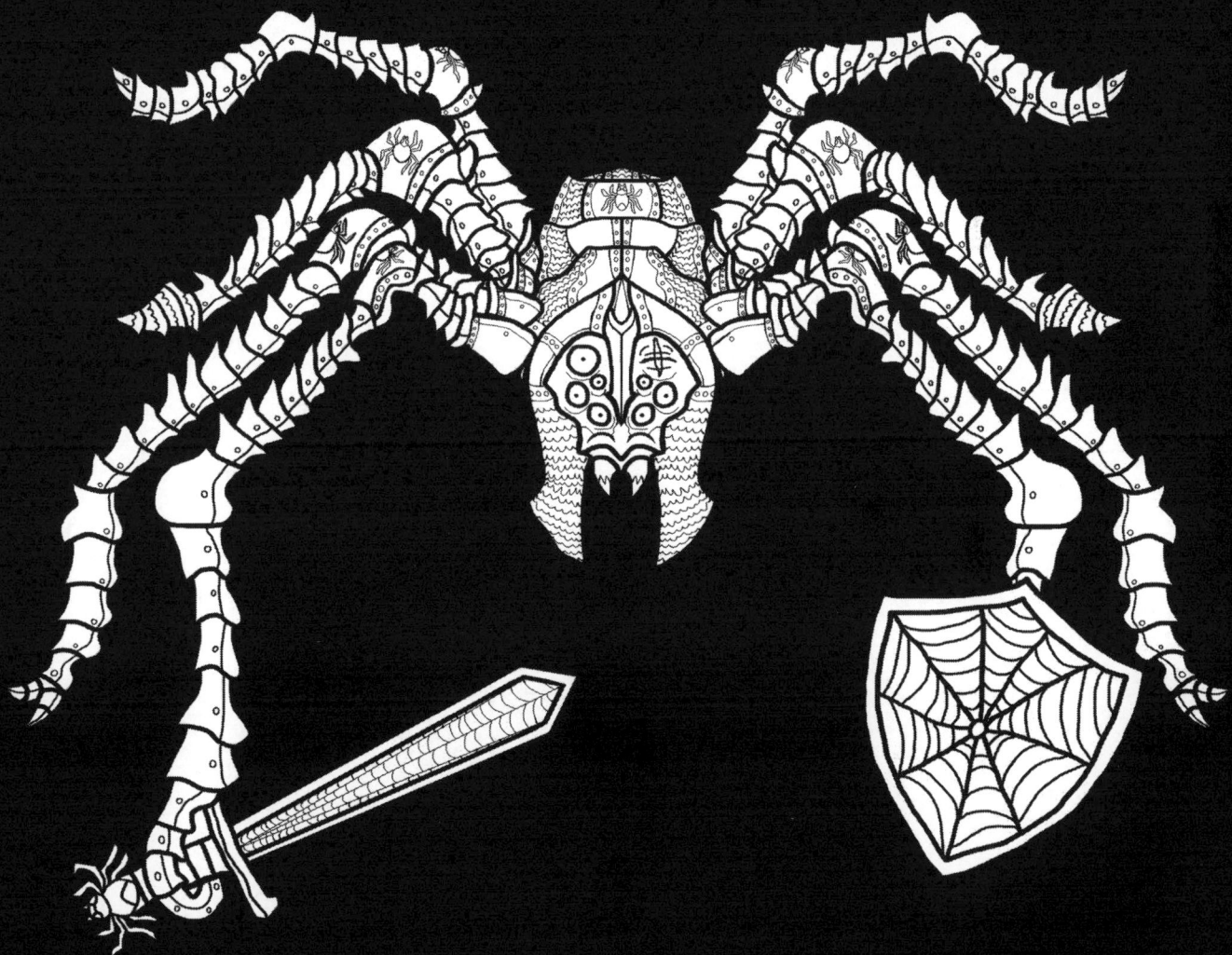

BOOKS IN THIS SERIES:

SHARE ONLINE
WE LOVE TO SEE YOUR COMPLETED MASTERPIECES

f FACEBOOK.COM/COLORING.BOOKS.FOR.GROWN.UPS/

OR

◉ @COMPLICATEDCOLORING

YOU CAN ALSO SHARE PHOTOS OF YOUR WORK IN AN AMAZON REVIEW.

VISIT OUR WEBSITE:
WWW.COMPLICATEDCOLORING.COM

FOR

UP-TO-DATE NEWS & RELEASES, T-SHIRTS, POSTERS & FREE PRINTABLE PAGES.

Printed in Great Britain
by Amazon